Published by Arbor Crest Publishing

Printed in the United States of America   July 2020–04

Table of Contents

Answer Section

$$\frac{10}{8} \quad \frac{2 \cdot 5}{2 \cdot 2 \cdot 2}$$

Finding the Slope of Linear Demand and Supply Curves

Question 1: Demand for Theater Tickets

Price	Quantity
$15.00	2
$5.00	10

$$\frac{\$15 - \$5}{2 - 10} = \frac{10}{-8}$$

$$\text{Slope} = -\frac{5}{4}$$

Question 2: Supply for Theater Tickets

Price	Quantity
$17.00	15
$2.00	2

$$\frac{\$17 - \$2}{15 - 2} = \frac{15}{13}$$

$$\text{Slope} = \frac{15}{13}$$

Given: In the summer, when concert tickets sell for $75, there are always 150,000 people that are willing and able to buy them, and the producers are willing and able to release 300,000 tickets. When the price falls to $50 a ticket, 75,000 more people are willing and able to buy them, but the producers are only willing and able to release 100,000 tickets.

Question 3: Demand for Concert Tickets

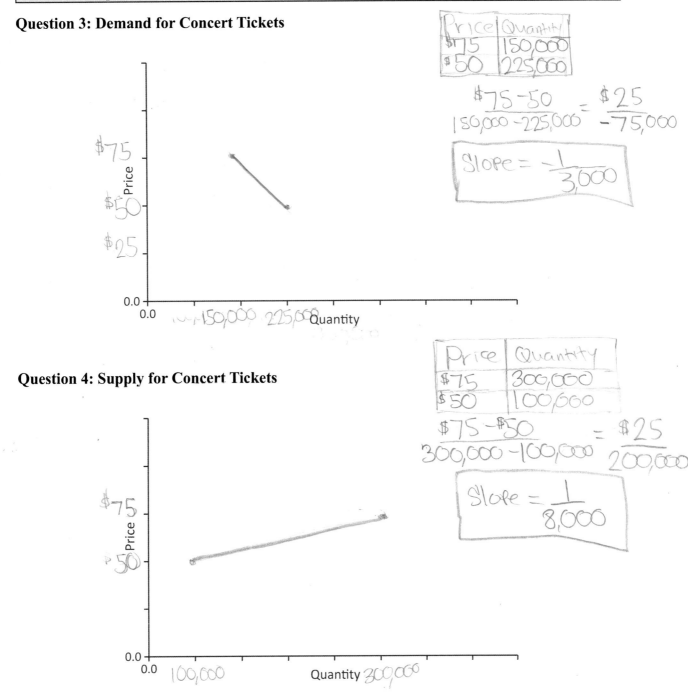

Price	Quantity
$75	150,000
$50	225,000

$$\frac{\$75-50}{150,000-225,000} = \frac{\$25}{-75,000}$$

$$Slope = -\frac{1}{3,000}$$

Question 4: Supply for Concert Tickets

Price	Quantity
$75	300,000
$50	100,000

$$\frac{\$75-\$50}{300,000-100,000} = \frac{\$25}{200,000}$$

$$Slope = \frac{1}{8,000}$$

Given: HP is trying to decide if they should run a 'Back-To-School' special on entry level computers. Estimate the slope of the annual supply & demand curves based on these quarterly price/quantity combinations.

Q1: $500	Q_D = 4.25 million	Q_S = 6.6 million
Q2: $700	Q_D = 3.75 million	Q_S = 7.5 million

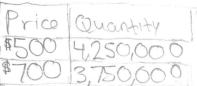

Price	Quantity
$500	4,250,000
$700	3,750,600

Question 5: Demand for HP Computers

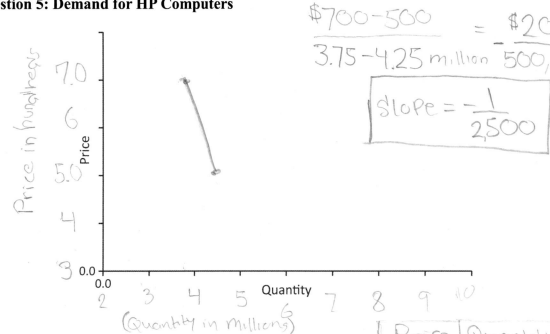

$$\frac{\$700-500}{3.75-4.25 \text{ million}} = \frac{\$200}{500,600}$$

$$\text{Slope} = -\frac{1}{2,500}$$

Question 6: Supply for HP Computers

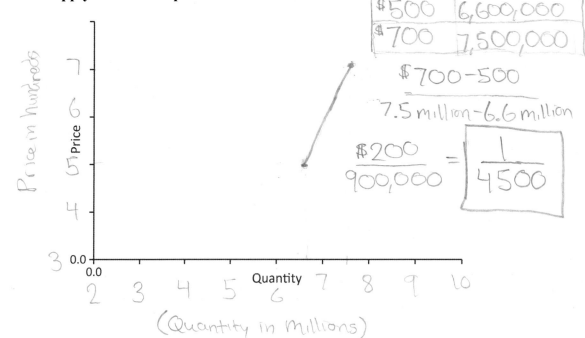

Price	Quantity
$500	6,600,000
$700	7,500,000

$$\frac{\$700-500}{7.5 \text{ million}-6.6 \text{ million}}$$

$$\frac{\$200}{900,000} = \frac{1}{4500}$$

Economics Workbook

Question 1: Germany and India only produce two goods. They have the same fixed resources, are equally efficient, and both countries have constant opportunity costs between the two goods. In one month, Germany can produce 200,000 automobiles or 60,000 hand-held computers. India can produce 150,000 automobiles or 50,000 hand-held computers.

A. Graph the given information.

B. What is the opportunity cost for Germany to produce automobiles?

$\frac{Computers}{Cars} \frac{60,000}{200,000}$ = Opportunity Cost of 1 Car is 0.3 Computers

C. What is the opportunity cost for India to produce automobiles?

$\frac{Computers}{Cars} \frac{50,000}{150,000}$ = Opportunity Cost of 1 Car is 0.333 computers

D. What is the opportunity cost for Germany to produce hand-held computers?

$\frac{Cars}{Computers} \frac{200,000}{60,000}$ = Opportunity Cost of 1 Computer is 3.3 Cars

E. What is the opportunity cost for India to produce hand-held computers?

$\frac{Cars}{Computers} \frac{150,000}{50,000}$ = Opportunity Cost of 1 computer is 3 Cars

F. Which nation has the absolute advantage in automobiles, which has the absolute advantage in hand-held computers?

Germany has the absolute advantage in both Cars (200,000) and computers (60,000)

G. Which nation has the comparative advantage in automobiles, which has the comparative advantage in hand-held computers? Germany has the comparative advantage in Cars, where they give up 0.3 Computers rather than 0.333

H. Can these nations benefit from trade? Explain how. Be detailed, use numbers and prove your answer.

Yes, since Germany benefits the most Producing Cars & india gains more producing hand-held Computers. Based on the data, Germany makes 50,000 more Cars than India & has a higher opportunity cost, where it must sacrifice more cars(3.3) to make a computer, than India. India, however, must give up more computers (0.333) for every Car.

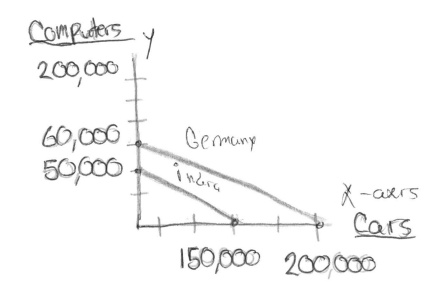

Solving for the equilibrium price (P*) and equilibrium quantity (Q*)

We know that equilibrium price and quantity clear the market. At one certain price, there will be no surplus or shortage. Supply and demand will be equal to each other. This means that we can solve for the equilibrium by setting the demand equation and the supply equation equal to each other. Once we find the equilibrium price, we can substitute it into either the supply equation or the demand equation and find out what the equilibrium quantity will be.

Question 1: Maria's Burrito Market

Demand = 100 – 6P
Supply = 28 + 3P

$D = 100 - 6(8)$
$D = 52$
$S = 28 + 3(8)$
$S = 52$

$100 - 6P = 28 + 3P$
$+6P = +6P$
$100 = 28 + 9P$
$-28 \quad -28$
$72 = 9P; \ P = 8$

$P = 8$
$D = 52$
$S = 52$

Question 2: Brushed Metal Watches Market

Demand = 1950 – 5P
Supply = 450 + 15P

$D = 1950 - 5(75)$
$D = 1575$
$S = 450 + 15(75)$
$S = 1575$

$1950 - 5P = 450 + 15P$
$-450 \qquad -450$
$1500 - 5P = 15P$
$+5P = 5P$
$1500 = 20P; \ P = 75$

$P = 75$
$D = 1575$
$S = 1575$

Question 3: Used Textbook Market

Demand = –3P + 270
Supply = 100 + 5P

$D = -3(21.25) + 270$
$D = 206.25$
$S = 100 + 5(21.25)$
$S = 206.25$

$-3P + 270 = 100 + 5P$
$-100 \qquad -100$
$-3P + 170 = 5P$
$+3P \qquad +3P$
$170 = 8P; \ P = 21.25$

$P = 21.25$
$D = 206.25$
$S = 206.25$

Question 4: Sunglass Market

This one is slightly different, but we know we are looking for the equilibrium quantity (Q^*) where Q_D is equal to Q_S. Since these two must represent the same number, we can call them both Q. The equations are both set to equal price, so we can set them equal to each other and solve as we have before.

Demand:	$P = 80 - Q_D$
Supply:	$P = 20 + 2Q_S$

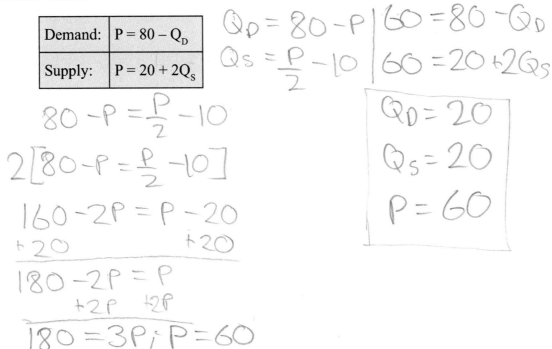

$$Q_D = 80 - P \mid 60 = 80 - Q_D$$
$$Q_S = \frac{P}{2} - 10 \mid 60 = 20 + 2Q_S$$

$$80 - P = \frac{P}{2} - 10$$

$$2\left[80 - P = \frac{P}{2} - 10\right]$$

$$160 - 2P = P - 20$$
$$\underline{+20 \qquad\qquad +20}$$
$$180 - 2P = P$$
$$\underline{+2P \quad +2P}$$
$$180 = 3P; \; P = 60$$

$$Q_D = 20$$
$$Q_S = 20$$
$$P = 60$$

Question 5: Sunglass Market with Taxes

What would happen if there was a tax on producers and they had to pay $6 for every pair of sunglasses that they sold? We would start with the same supply and demand curve from above, but we would decrease the seller's price by the amount of the tax.

Demand:	$P = 80 - Q_D$
Supply:	$P-6 = 20 + 2Q_S \rightarrow P = 26 + 2Q_S$

$$80 - Q = 26 + 2Q$$
$$\underline{+Q \qquad\qquad +Q}$$
$$80 = 26 + 3Q$$
$$\underline{-26 \quad -26}$$
$$54 = 3Q; \; Q = 18$$

$$D = 80 - 18$$
$$D = 62$$

$$S = 26 + 2(18)$$
$$S = 62$$

$$Q = 18$$
$$D = 62$$
$$S = 62$$

Question 6: DVD Recorder Market, quantity in thousands

Demand:	$P = 150 - 3Q_D$
Supply:	$P = 90 + 5Q_S$

$$150 - 3Q = 90 + 5Q$$
$$\underline{-90 \qquad\quad -90}$$
$$60 - 3Q = 5Q$$
$$\underline{+3Q \quad +3Q}$$
$$60 = 8Q; \; Q = 7.5$$

$$D = 150 - 3(7.5)$$
$$P = 127.5$$
$$S = 90 + 5(7.5)$$
$$S = 127.5$$

$$Q = 7.5 \, (7,500)$$
$$D = 127.5$$
$$S = 127.5$$

Question 7: DVD Recorder Market with Taxes

What would happen if there was a tax on selling DVD Recorders of $17? We would start with the same supply and demand curve from above, but we would decrease the seller's price by the amount of the tax.

Demand:	$P = 150 - 3Q_D$
Supply:	$P - 17 = 90 + 5Q_S \rightarrow P = 107 + 5Q_S$

**How much did the government received in tax revenue?

$$150 - 3Q = 107 + 5Q$$
$$\underline{-107 \qquad\quad -107}$$
$$43 - 3Q = 5Q$$
$$\underline{+3Q \quad = +3Q}$$
$$43 = 8Q; \; Q = 5.375$$
$$Q = 5,375$$
$$5,375 \times \$17 = \$91,375$$

$$D = 150 - 3(5.375)$$
$$D = 133.875$$
$$S = 107 + 5(5.375)$$
$$S = 133.875$$

$$Q = 5.375 \, (5,375)$$
$$D = 133.875$$
$$S = 133.875$$
$$R = \$91,375$$

Basic Elasticity Word Problems

1. Anna owns the Sweet Alps Chocolate store. She charges $10 per pound for her hand made chocolate. You, the economist, have calculated the elasticity of demand for chocolate in her town to be 2.5. If she wants to increase her total revenue, what advice will you give her and why? Be able to explain your answer.

2. If the cross elasticity of demand between peanut butter and milk is –1.11, then are peanut butter and milk substitutes or complements? Be able to explain your answer.

3. A 10 percent increase in income brings about a 15 percent decrease in the demand for a good. What is the income elasticity of demand and is the good a normal good or an inferior good? Be able to explain your answer.

4. If the price of a good increases by 8% and the quantity demanded decreases by 12%, what is the price elasticity of demand? Is it elastic, inelastic or unitary elastic?

5. Discount stores sell relatively elastic goods. *Ceteris paribus,* explain why selling at a relatively low price is profitable for them?

Mathematical Elasticity Questions

Question 1: It is barrel tasting in the Wine County (let's assume this means people buy wine by the barrel). One of the wineries realized that if they sell their barrels for $450 they sold 137,500 barrels over the weekend. If they decrease their price to $375 they would sell 27,500 more.

A. What is the arc elasticity over the relevant range?

B. What happens to total revenue with the price reduction?

C. Graph this problem.

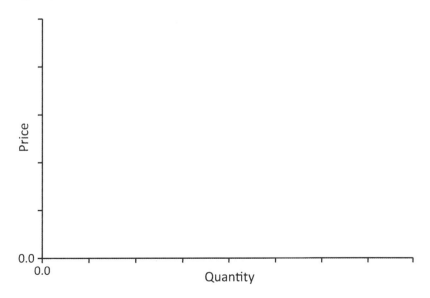

Question 2: Donna Mia's is currently selling their dinner specials for $13.00 each. The restaurant is thinking about increasing that price by $2.00. They hired an economist to figure out how that would affect total revenue which is currently one hundred and fifty-six thousand dollars a month. The economist estimated that total revenue would fall by about 3.846 percent.

A. What is the price elasticity of demand over the relevant range?

B. How many dinners will be sold at the new price?

C. Explain why this would/would not be a good idea. You must use the elasticity coefficient (explain what the number means), total revenue, and what you know about price elasticity of demand to support your answer.

D. Graph this problem.

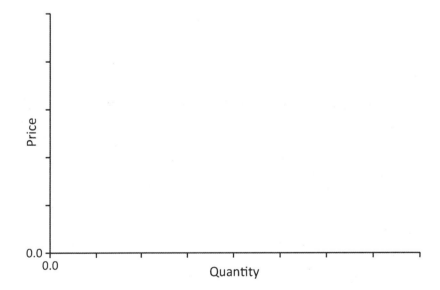

Question 3: The Droid and the iPhone are both smart cellular phones with web based applications. They are known to have a cross price elasticity of 2.0. Apple currently sells three million of the cheapest iPhone for $200. The Droid came out and was selling for $150, but Verizon wants to reduce the price to $135.

A. Calculate how many iPhones Apple should expect to sell and what will happen to their total revenue.

B. Use two graphs (one for the iPhone and one for Droid) to show the effects of this change of prices.

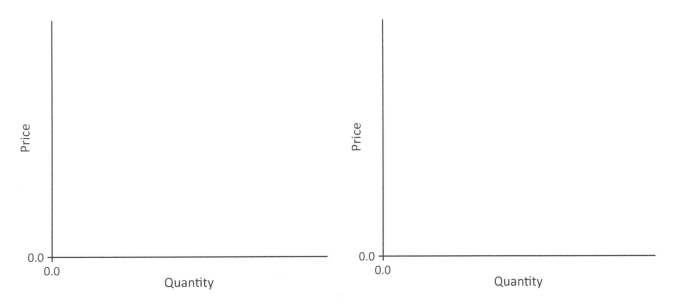

C. Explain how these two goods are related. You must include the explanation of the elasticity coefficient, and what it means.

Question 4: Since the economy has been in a recession, the average consumer's income has gone from $44,375 to $41,720. Before the recession, XYZ Auto Row was selling a combined 600 vehicles per month. As an economist, predict the number of vehicles they will sell for the following income elasticities, and explain what type of good automobiles are in the eyes of consumers (you must use explain what the elasticity coefficient means).

A. $E_I = 1.5$

B. $E_I = .5$

C. $E_I = -2$

Question 5: Graph the demand curve for these statements and calculate the arc elasticity coefficient. Label everything. Use one graph per statement.

A. I really like my girlfriend and will take her to the movies every week.

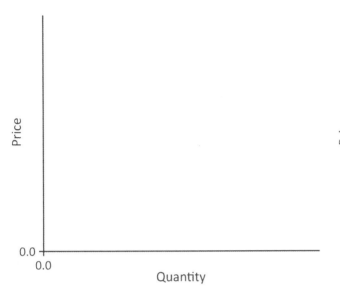

B. If we go to the $5.00 matinee, I will take my girlfriend and her 3 sisters. If we go in the evening for $7, it will be just the two of us.

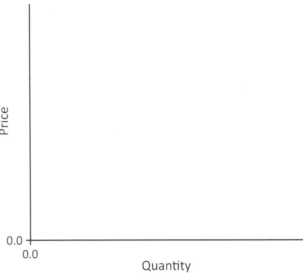

C. I bought a Costco gift card and will spend $25 on going to the movies.

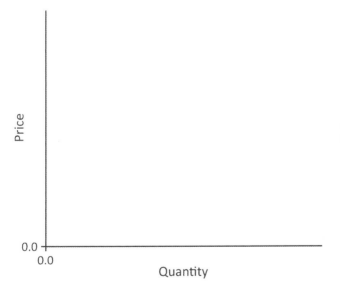

D. I will always take my girlfriend to the movies, as long as the price isn't over $9.75

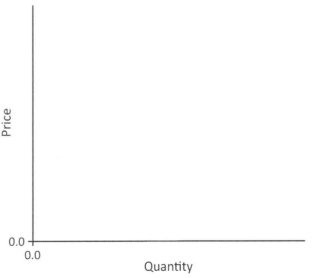

Question 6: U2 just came out with a new album. They have been selling 10,000 CDs a month at $15.00. Since Coldplay is also releasing a new album, U2 is considering selling their CD at $13.00. U2 hired an economist and found the price elasticity of demand to be (–) 1.5 over the relevant range.

A. Graph the question.

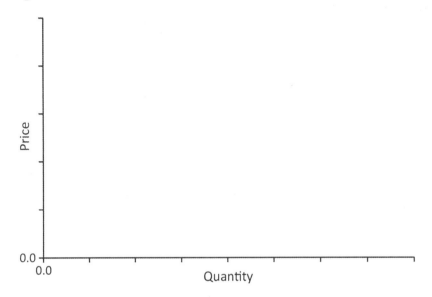

B. How many CDs should U2 expect to sell if they change the price?

C. Use total revenue to explain if this is a good economic decision.

Question 7: The Oakland A's and the San Francisco Giants are two Major League Baseball teams that have ballparks located with in 16 miles of each other. The San Francisco Giants are currently selling 20,000 club level seats at $35.00 each for their home games. The Oakland A's were selling their club level seats for $25.00, but are going to reduce the price to $20.00. An economist found the cross-price elasticity to be 3.0 between the two team's club level seats.

A. Graph the given information.

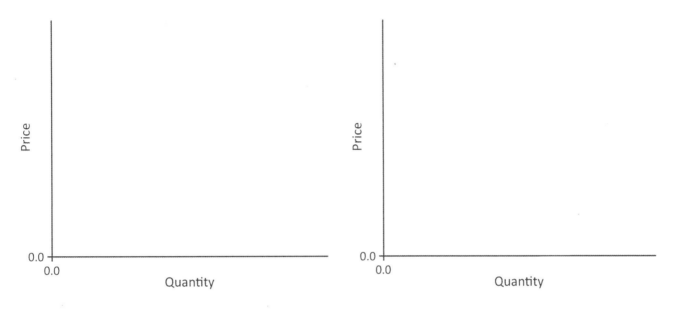

B. Calculate how many seats the SF Giants should expect to sell with the A's new price.

C. Use the coefficient to explain how these two goods are related.

Question 8: Wally's World of Widgets hires you as their full time economist. After studying their business, you realize that when the price of Widgets are $50.00 they sell 20,000 units a month and when they put Widgets on sale for $35.00 they sell 10,000 units more a month.

A. Graph the given information.

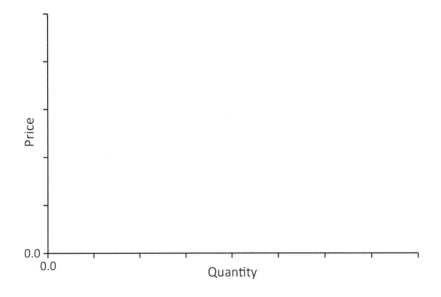

B. What is the arc elasticity over the relevant range? What does this number mean?

C. Use total revenue to explain if this is a good economic decision.

Question 1: Use the graph to answer the following questions. All labels have been removed, but you can assume that the supply and demand curves are the same ones that we have been working with for most of the semester, you can also assume that the axis are the ones that we typically have used (price is in dollars and quantity is in thousands).

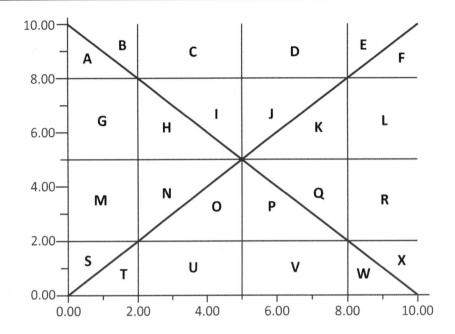

In equilibrium, what are the letters and the total dollar amounts that correspond to the area for the...

i. Original Consumer Surplus?

ii. Original Producer Surplus?

iii. Total Market Surplus?

Assume an effective quota has been placed on the market, changing the quantity by 3,000 units. What are the letters and the total dollar amounts that now correspond to the...

iv. New Consumer Surplus?

v. New Producer Surplus?

vi. Area that was transferred?

vii. Dead Weight Loss?

viii. Remaining Surplus?

Finding the Slope of Linear Demand and Supply Curves
Question 1: Demand for Theater Tickets

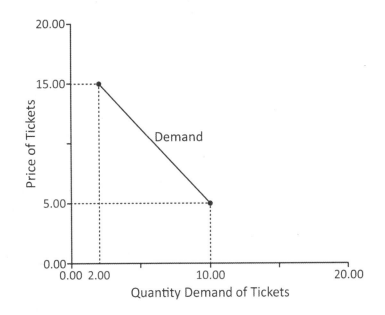

Price	Quantity
$15.00	2
$5.00	10

$$\frac{\Delta P}{\Delta Q} \qquad \frac{\$15 - \$5}{2 - 10}$$

$$\textbf{Slope}: \quad -\frac{5}{4}$$

Question 2: Supply for Theater Tickets

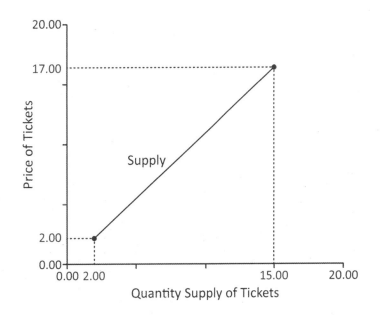

Price	Quantity
$17.00	15
$2.00	2

$$\frac{\Delta P}{\Delta Q} \qquad \frac{\$17 - \$2}{15 - 2}$$

$$\textbf{Slope}: \quad \frac{15}{13}$$

Given: In the summer, when concert tickets sell for $75, there are always 150,000 people that are willing and able to buy them, and the producers are willing and able to release 300,000 tickets. When the price falls to $50 a ticket, 75,000 more people are willing and able to buy them, but the producers are only willing and able to release 100,000 tickets.

Question 3: Demand for Concert Tickets

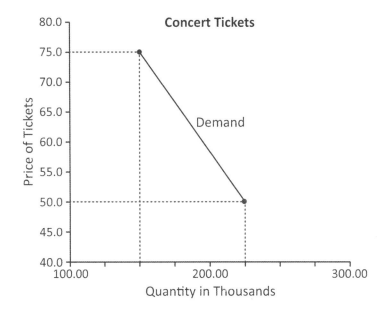

Price	Quantity
$75.00	150,000
$50.00	225,000

$$\frac{\Delta P}{\Delta Q} \qquad \frac{\$75 - \$50}{150,000 - 225,000}$$

$$\textbf{Slope:} \quad \frac{25}{-75,000} = -\frac{1}{3,000}$$

Question 4: Supply for Concert Tickets

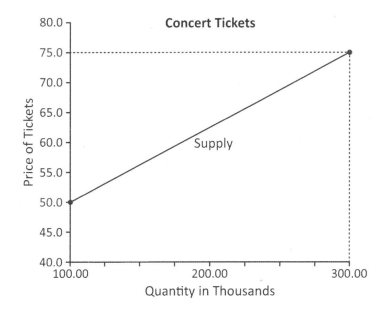

Price	Quantity
$75.00	300,000
$50.00	100,000

$$\frac{\Delta P}{\Delta Q} \qquad \frac{\$75 - \$50}{300,000 - 100,000}$$

$$\textbf{Slope:} \quad \frac{25}{200,000} = \frac{1}{8,000}$$

Given: HP is trying to decide if they should run a 'Back-To-School' special on entry level computers. Estimate the slope of the annual supply & demand curves based on these quarterly price/quantity combinations.

Q1: $500	$Q_D = 4.25_{million}$	$Q_S = 6.6_{million}$
Q2: $700	$Q_D = 3.75_{million}$	$Q_S = 7.5_{million}$

Question 5: Demand for HP Computers

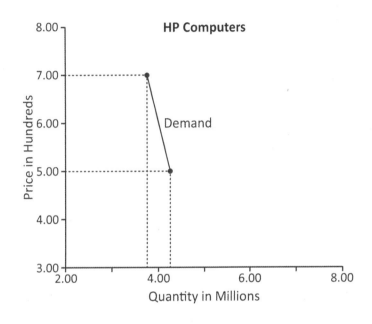

Price	Quantity
$700	3,750,000
$500	4,250,000

$$\frac{\Delta P}{\Delta Q} \qquad \frac{\$700 - \$500}{3.75_{million} - 4.25_{million}}$$

$$\text{Slope:} \qquad \frac{200}{-500,000} = -\frac{1}{2,500}$$

Question 6: Supply for HP Computers

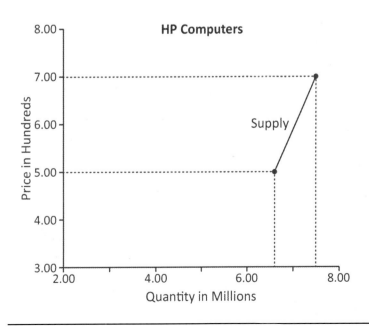

Price	Quantity
$700	7,500,000
$500	6,600,000

$$\frac{\Delta P}{\Delta Q} \qquad \frac{\$700 - \$500}{7.5_{million} - 6.6_{million}}$$

$$\text{Slope:} \qquad \frac{200}{900,000} = \frac{1}{4,500}$$

Question 1: Germany and India only produce two goods. They have the same fixed resources, are equally efficient, and both countries have constant opportunity costs between the two goods. In one month, Germany can produce 200,000 automobiles or 60,000 hand-held computers. India can produce 150,000 automobiles or 50,000 hand-held computers.

A. Graph the given information.

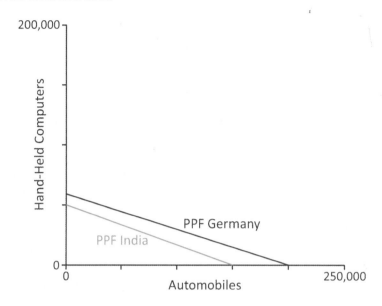

B. What is the opportunity cost for Germany to produce automobiles?

$$1 \text{ Automobile} = \frac{60,000 \text{ Computers}}{200,000 \text{ Automobiles}} \rightarrow \textbf{Opportunity Cost for 1 auto is 0.3 computers}$$

C. What is the opportunity cost for India to produce automobiles?

$$1 \text{ Automobile} = \frac{50,000 \text{ Computers}}{150,000 \text{ Automobiles}} \rightarrow \textbf{Opportunity Cost for 1 auto is 0.333 computers}$$

D. What is the opportunity cost for Germany to produce hand-held computers?

$$1 \text{ Computer} = \frac{200,000 \text{ Automobiles}}{60,000 \text{ Computers}} \rightarrow \textbf{Opportunity Cost for 1 computer is 3.3 autos}$$

E. What is the opportunity cost for India to produce hand-held computers?

$$1 \text{ Computer} = \frac{150,000 \text{ Automobiles}}{50,000 \text{ Computers}} \rightarrow \textbf{Opportunity Cost for 1 computer is 3.0 autos}$$

F. **Which nation has the absolute advantage in automobiles, which has the absolute advantage in hand-held computers?**

Germany has the absolute advantage in the production of both goods.

G. **Which nation has the comparative advantage in automobiles, which has the comparative advantage in hand-held computers?**

Germany has the comparative advantage in automobiles, since they are giving up 0.3 computers for every car that they make and India is giving up 0.33 computers.

India has the comparative advantage in hand-held computers, since they are giving up only 3.0 cars for every computer they make, where Germany is giving up 3.33 cars.

H. **Can these nations benefit from trade? Explain how. Be detailed, use numbers and prove your answer.**

Yes, both nations can be better off with specialization and trade. If Germany produces 200,000 cars and India produces 50,000 computers, they would both be willing to enter a trade agreement as long as Germany was getting more than 0.3 computers for every car and India was getting more than 3 cars for each computer.

Solving for the equilibrium price (P*) and equilibrium quantity (Q*)

> We know that equilibrium price and quantity clear the market. At one certain price, there will be no surplus or shortage. Supply and demand will be equal to each other. This means that we can solve for the equilibrium by setting the demand equation and the supply equation equal to each other. Once we find the equilibrium price, we can substitute it into either the supply equation or the demand equation and find out what the equilibrium quantity will be.

Question 1: Maria's Burrito Market

Demand = 100 – 6P
Supply = 28 + 3P

$100 - 6P = 28 + 3P$

$100 - 28 = 6P + 3P$

$72 = 9P$

$\dfrac{72}{9} = P$

$P^* = \$8.00$

Demand $= 100 - 6P$	Supply $= 28 + 3P$
Demand $= 100 - 6(8)$	Supply $= 28 + 3(8)$
Demand $= 100 - 48$	Supply $= 28 + 24$
Demand = 52	**Supply = 52**

Question 2: Brushed Metal Watches Market

Demand = 1950 – 5P
Supply = 450 + 15P

$1950 - 5P = 450 + 15P$

$1950 - 450 = 5P + 15P$

$1500 = 20P$

$\dfrac{1500}{20} = P$

$P^* = \$75.00$

Demand $= 1950 - 5P$	Supply $= 450 + 15P$
Demand $= 1950 - 5(75)$	Supply $= 450 + 15(75)$
Demand $= 1950 - 375$	Supply $= 450 + 1125$
Demand = 1575	**Supply = 1575**

Question 3: Used Textbook Market

| Demand = −3P + 270 |
| Supply = 100 + 5P |

$-3p + 270 = 100 + 5P$

$170 = 8P$

P* = $21.25

Demand = −3P + 270	Supply = 100 + 5P
Demand = −3(21.25) + 270	Supply = 100 + 5(21.25)
Demand = −63.75 + 270	Supply = 100 + 106.25
Demand = 206.25	**Supply = 206.25**

Question 4: Sunglass Market

This one is slightly different, but we know we are looking for the equilibrium quantity (Q*) where Q_D is equal to Q_S. Since these two must represent the same number, we can call them both Q. The equations are both set to equal price, so we can set them equal to each other and solve as we have before.

Demand:	$P = 80 - Q_D$
Supply:	$P = 20 + 2Q_S$

$80 - Q = 20 + 2Q$

$60 = 3Q$

Q* = 20

Demand : P = 80 − Q	Supply : P = 20 + 2Q
Demand : P = 80 − (20)	Supply : P = 20 + 2(20)
Demand : P = 60	**Supply : P = 60**

Question 5: Sunglass Market with Taxes

What would happen if there was a tax on producers and they had to pay $6 for every pair of sunglasses that they sold? We would start with the same supply and demand curve from above, but we would decrease the seller's price by the amount of the tax.

Demand:	$P = 80 - Q_D$
Supply:	$P-6 = 20 + 2Q_S \rightarrow P = 26 + 2Q_S$

$80 - Q = 26 + 2Q$

$54 = 3Q$

Q* = 18

Demand : P = 80 − Q	Supply : P − 6 = 20 + 2Q
Demand : P = 80 − (18)	Supply : P − 6 = 20 + 2(18)
Demand : P = 62 (including tax)	**Supply : P = 62 (including tax)**

Question 6: DVD Recorder Market, quantity in thousands

Demand:	$P = 150 - 3Q_D$
Supply:	$P = 90 + 5Q_S$

$150 - 3Q = 90 + 5Q$

$60 = 8Q$

$Q^* = 7.5$ **(7,500 sold)**

Demand: $P = 150 - 3Q_D$	Supply: $P = 90 + 5Q_S$
Demand: $P = 150 - 3(7.5)$	Supply: $P = 90 + 5(7.5)$
Demand: $P^* = 127.5$	**Supply: $P^* = 127.5$**

Question 7: DVD Recorder Market with Taxes

What would happen if there was a tax on selling DVD Recorders of $17? We would start with the same supply and demand curve from above, but we would decrease the seller's price by the amount of the tax.

Demand:	$P = 150 - 3Q_D$
Supply:	$P{-}17 = 90 + 5Q_S \rightarrow P = 107 + 5Q_S$

$150 - 3Q = 170 + 5Q$

$43 = 8Q$

$Q^* = 5.375$ **(5,375 sold)**

Demand: $P = 150 - 3Q_D$	Supply: $P = 107 + 5Q_S$
Demand: $P = 150 - 3(5.375)$	Supply: $P = 107 + 5(5.375)$
Demand: $P = 133.875$ (inc. tax)	**Supply: $P = 133.875$ (inc. tax)**

**How much did the government received in tax revenue?

The government receives $17 for each unit sold. The quantity was 5.375 (in thousands).
Q* = 5,375
Tax = $17
Government Revenue: $91,375

Basic Elasticity Word Problems

1. **Anna owns the Sweet Alps Chocolate store. She charges $10 per pound for her hand made chocolate. You, the economist, have calculated the elasticity of demand for chocolate in her town to be 2.5. If she wants to increase her total revenue, what advice will you give her and why? Be able to explain your answer.**

   Anna should lower her price. Her price elasticity of demand for chocolate is elastic (greater than one) and therefore, when she lowers her price she will sell a lot more chocolate. The greater quantity sold will make up for her lower price, increasing her total revenue. In other words, she is selling at a lower price but making up for it in volume of sales.

2. **If the cross elasticity of demand between peanut butter and milk is –1.11, then are peanut butter and milk substitutes or complements? Be able to explain your answer.**

   Peanut butter and milk are complements because a negative cross price elasticity of demand means that as the price of milk goes up, the demand for peanut butter goes down. This would indicate that when the price of milk goes up, we buy less milk and we are also buying less peanut butter (so we must buy these together — they are complements).

3. **A 10 percent increase in income brings about a 15 percent decrease in the demand for a good. What is the income elasticity of demand and is the good a normal good or an inferior good? Be able to explain your answer.**

   $-15\%/10\% = -.15/.10 = -1.5$. Remember the elasticity is always read as the absolute value or a positive number, so it is 1.5 (elastic, or greater than one). The good is an inferior good because the sign is negative, indicating that an increase in income will bring a decrease in the demand for the good.

4. **If the price of a good increases by 8% and the quantity demanded decreases by 12%, what is the price elasticity of demand? Is it elastic, inelastic or unitary elastic?**

   $-12\%/8\% = -.12/.08 = -1.5$. Again, drop the negative sign, so the elasticity is 1.5. This means it is elastic (greater than one).

5. **Discount stores sell relatively elastic goods.** *Ceteris paribus,* **explain why selling at a relatively low price is profitable for them?**

   It is profitable because with elastic goods, dropping the price lower can bring them a lot more business. Therefore, at the low prices they can sell a large volume of goods, making up for the lower prices and bringing in more revenue (P x Q).

Mathematical Elasticity Questions

> **Question 1:** It is barrel tasting in the Wine County (let's assume this means people buy wine by the barrel). One of the wineries realized that if they sell their barrels for $450 they sold 137,500 barrels over the weekend. If they decrease their price to $375 they would sell 27,500 more.

Let's take a moment to write down the important information from the problem:

P1: $450	Q1: 137,500	TR1: P1 * Q1
P2: $375	Q2: 165,000	TR2: P2 * Q2

A. What is the arc elasticity over the relevant range?

$$Ep = \frac{\dfrac{Q2-Q1}{Q2+Q1}}{\dfrac{P2-P1}{P2+P1}} \rightarrow \frac{\dfrac{165,000-137,500}{165,000+137,500}}{\dfrac{\$375-\$450}{\$375+\$450}} \rightarrow \frac{\dfrac{27,500}{202,000}}{\dfrac{-75}{827}} \rightarrow \frac{0.0906}{-0.0906} \rightarrow -1.0 \boxed{\textbf{Unit Elastic}}$$

OR :

$$Ep = \frac{\dfrac{\Delta Q}{\dfrac{(Q2+Q1)}{2}}}{\dfrac{\Delta P}{\dfrac{(P2+P1)}{2}}} \rightarrow \frac{\dfrac{-27,500}{151,250}}{\dfrac{\$75}{\$412.50}} \rightarrow \frac{0.181818}{0.181818} \rightarrow -1.0 \boxed{\textbf{Unit Elastic}}$$

B. What happens to total revenue with the price reduction?

Since we know that the barrels are unitary elastic, if they winery increases their price by 5%, their sales will fall by 5%. If they decrease their price by 10 %, their sales will fall by 10% and there will not be a net change to total revenue. We can check this by plugging in the numbers from the problem. If total revenue does not change, it confirms that the math above is correct and the winery's product is in fact unitary elastic.

TR1: (P1 * Q1)	TR2: (P2 * Q2)
TR1: $450 (137, 500)	TR2: $375 (165,000)
TR1: $61,875,000	TR2: $61,875,000

C. Graph this problem.

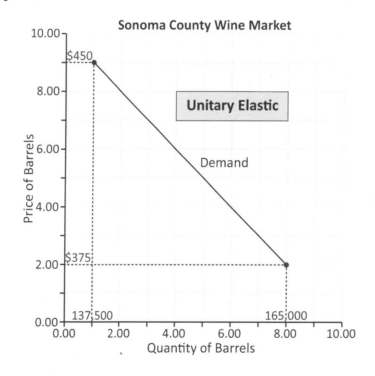

> **Question 2:** Donna Mia's is currently selling their dinner specials for $13.00 each. The restaurant is thinking about increasing that price by $2.00. They hired an economist to figure out how that would affect total revenue which is currently one hundred and fifty-six thousand dollars a month. The economist estimated that total revenue would fall by about 3.846 percent.

We start by writing down what we know from the information above.

P1: $13.00	Q1: $156,000/$13 = 12,000	TR1: $ 156,000
P2: $15.00	Q2: ???	TR2: $ 156,000 − 3.846% → $150,000

A. What is the price elasticity of demand over the relevant range?

$$Ep = \frac{\dfrac{Q2-Q1}{Q1}}{\dfrac{P2-P1}{P1}} \rightarrow \frac{\dfrac{10,000-12,000}{12,000}}{\dfrac{\$15-\$13}{\$13}} \rightarrow \frac{\dfrac{-2,000}{12,000}}{\dfrac{\$2}{\$13}} \rightarrow \frac{0.16667}{0.15385} \rightarrow -1.08$$

We could use also use arc elasticity to solve this. The number would not be as precise.

$$Ep = \frac{\dfrac{Q2-Q1}{Q2+q1}}{\dfrac{P2-P1}{P2+P1}} \rightarrow \frac{\dfrac{10,000-12,000}{10,000+12,000}}{\dfrac{\$15-\$13}{\$15+\$13}} \rightarrow \frac{\dfrac{-2,000}{22,000}}{\dfrac{\$2}{\$28}} \rightarrow \frac{-0.09}{0.07} \rightarrow -1.285$$

OR :

$$Ep = \frac{\dfrac{\Delta Q}{\dfrac{(Q2+Q1)}{2}}}{\dfrac{\Delta P}{\dfrac{(P2+P1)}{2}}} \rightarrow \frac{\dfrac{-2,000}{\dfrac{11,000}{2}}}{\dfrac{14}{ }} \rightarrow \frac{0.181818}{0.142857} \rightarrow -1.27$$

B. How many dinners will be sold at the new price?

We know that the new total revenue (TR2) will fall by 3.846%, when the price changes to $15, so we only have to divide the new total revenue by the new price.

P2: $15.00   TR2: $ 156,000 − 3.846% = $150,000 → Q2: $150,000/$15 → **10,000**

C. Explain why this would/would not be a good idea. You must use the elasticity coefficient (explain what the number means), total revenue, and what you know about price elasticity of demand to support your answer.

Since the price elasticity of demand is –1.08 (or –1.3 with arc elasticity), it is in the elastic range. Consumers are relatively sensitive to changes in price. The coefficient tells us for every 1% increase in price, there will be a 1.08% (~1.3%) decrease in the quantity demanded. That means that total revenue will fall by $6000.00 if they increase the price of the dinners by $2.00.

D. Graph this problem.

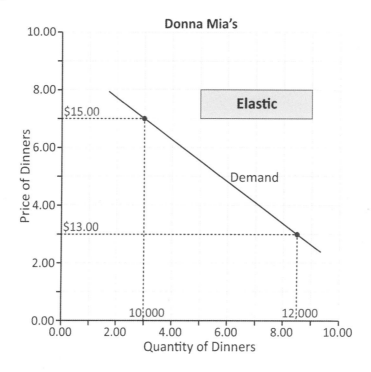

Question 3: The Droid and the iPhone are both smart cellular phones with web based applications. They are known to have a cross price elasticity of 2.0. Apple currently sells three million of the cheapest iPhone for $200. The Droid came out and was selling for $150, but Verizon wants to reduce the price to $135.

PY1: $150.00	QDX1: 3,000,000	EXY: 2.0
PY2: $135.00	QDX2:???	

A. Calculate how many iPhones Apple should expect to sell and what will happen to their total revenue.

This is the formula for cross-price elasticity. It looks at the percent change in quantity demanded of one good (iPhones), with respect to the percent change in price of the other good (Droids).

$$EXY = \frac{\% \Delta QDX}{\% \Delta PY}$$

$$2.0 = \frac{\% \Delta QDX}{\frac{(150-135)}{150}} \rightarrow 2.0 = \frac{\% \Delta QDX}{10\%} \rightarrow \% \Delta QDX = 20$$

Now that we know that the percent change in the quantity demanded of the iPhone will be 20%, we can subtract 20% from the original quantity of iPhones (Qx1) to find the new quantity (Qx2).

$$Q \times 2 = Q \times 1 - 20\% \rightarrow 3,000,000 - 20\% = \mathbf{2,400,000}$$

To find out what the new total revenue is for Apple, we take the new quantity (Qx2) and multiply it by the price of iPhones (remember this price has not changed).

$$TR2 = \$200 \times 2,400,000 = \$480,000,000$$
$$\Delta TR : \$600,000,000 - \$480,000,000 = \mathbf{\$120,000,000}$$

Using the same formula for cross-price elasticity, we can also find the new quantity by plugging in our know values instead of calculating percentages.

$$EXY = \frac{\%\Delta QDX}{\%\Delta PY}$$

$$2.0 = \frac{\dfrac{QX2 - QX1}{QX2 + QX1}}{\dfrac{PY2 - PY1}{PY2 + PY1}} \rightarrow \frac{\dfrac{QX2 - 3,000,000}{QX2 + 3,000,000}}{\dfrac{\$135 - \$150}{\$135 + \$150}} \rightarrow \frac{\dfrac{QX2 - 3,000,000}{QX2 + 3,000,000}}{\dfrac{-\$15.00}{\$285.00}}$$

$$2.0 = \frac{QX2 - 3,000,000}{QX2 + 3,000,000} \times \frac{\$285.00}{-\$15.00}$$

$$2.0 = \frac{285(QX2 - 3,000,000)}{-15(QX2 + 3,000,000)}$$

$$285QX2 - 855,000,000 = 2(-15QX2 - 45,000,000)$$
$$285QX2 - 855,000,000 = -30QX2 - 90,000,000$$
$$315QX2 = 765,000,000$$
$$QX2 = \mathbf{2,428,571}$$

$$TR1: (\$200.00 \times 3,000,000) = \$600,000,000$$
$$TR2: (\$200.00 \times 2,428,571) = \$485,714,200$$
$$\Delta TR: \$600,000,000 - \$485,714,200 = \mathbf{\$114,285,714}$$

B. Use two graphs (one for the iPhone and one for Droid) to show the effects of this change of prices.

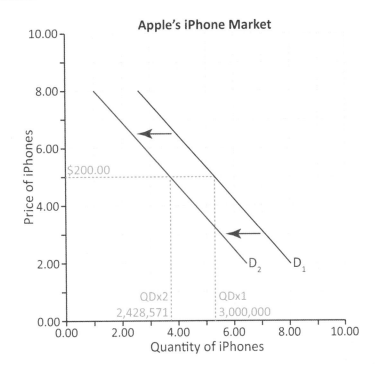

Apple's iPhone Market

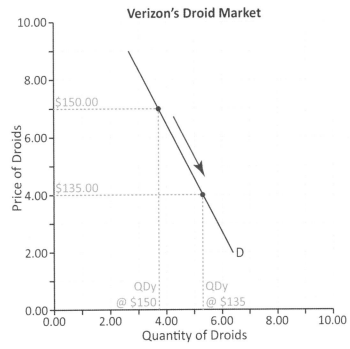

Verizon's Droid Market

C. Explain how these two goods are related. You must include the explanation of the elasticity coefficient, and what it means.

The cross-price elasticity of iPhones and Droids are **positive**, so consumers view them as **substitutes**. The coefficient of 2.0 means that for every **1% decrease in the price of Droids, the quantity demanded of iPhones will fall by 2%**.

> **Question 4:** Since the economy has been in a recession, the average consumer's income has gone from $44,375 to $41,720. Before the recession, XYZ Auto Row was selling a combined 600 vehicles per month. As an economist, predict the number of vehicles they will sell for the following income elasticities, and explain what type of good automobiles are in the eyes of consumers (you must use explain what the elasticity coefficient means).

A. $E_I = 1.5$

B. $E_I = .5$

C. $E_I = -2$

Start with what we know, and what we are trying to figure out.

Income 1: $44,375	Q1: 600
Income 2: $41,720	Q2: ???

The first thing that we need to find out how much income has changed by.

$$\%\Delta I = \frac{41,720 - 44,375}{44,375} = -0.059$$

Now that we have the percentage, we can plug that into the bottom of the income elasticity formula. The different levels of income elasticity are given, so once we plug that in we will just be solving for the new quantity.

This is the income elasticity formula:

$$E_I = \frac{\%\Delta QD}{\%\Delta I}$$

A. $E_I = 1.5$

$$1.5 = \frac{X}{-0.059} \rightarrow 1.5(-0.06) = -0.9$$

This means that quantity demanded will fall by 9%. We now need to see how many cars they will sell, buy subtracting 9% from the amount they sold before the recession.

$$600 - 9\% \rightarrow 600 \times -0.9 = -54$$

$$600 - 54 = \boxed{\textbf{546 Cars}}$$

$E_I = 1.5$ means that consumers see this good as a luxury item, and that for every 1% change in their income, they will respond with a 1.5% change in quantity demanded. Consumer income fell by roughly 6%, and the quantity demanded fell by 9%.

B. $E_I = .5$

We just plug our E_I of .5 into our formula:

$$E_I = \frac{\%\Delta QD}{\%\Delta I}$$

$$.5 = \frac{\%\Delta QD}{-0.059} \quad \rightarrow \quad .5(-0.06) = -0.03$$

This means that quantity demanded will fall by 3%. We now need to see how many cars they will sell, buy subtracting 3% from the amount they sold before the recession.

$$600 - 3\% \quad \rightarrow \quad 600 \times -0.03 = -18$$

$$600 - 18 = \boxed{\textbf{582 Cars}}$$

$E_I = .5$ means that consumers see this good as a basic, normal item, and that for every 1% change in their income, they will respond with a .5% change in quantity demanded. Consumer income fell by roughly 6%, and the quantity demanded fell by 3%.

C. $E_I = -2$

$$-2 = \frac{\%\Delta QD}{-0.059} \quad \rightarrow \quad -2(-0.06) = (+).12$$

Since our income elasticity was a negative number, we have quantity demanded increasing by 12%. We now need to see how many cars they will sell, buy adding 12% to the amount they sold before the recession.

$$600 + 12\% \quad \rightarrow \quad 600 \times .12 = 72$$

$$600 + 72 = \boxed{\textbf{672 Cars}}$$

$E_I = -2$ means that consumers see this good as an inferior item. When incomes go down, they start buying more of this type of good. Here, for every 1% change in their income, they will respond with a 2% change in quantity demanded.

Consumer income fell by roughly 6%, and the quantity demanded <u>increased</u> by 12%.

Question 5: Graph the demand curve for these statements and calculate the arc elasticity coefficient. Label everything. Use one graph per statement.

A. I really like my girlfriend and will take her to the movies every week.

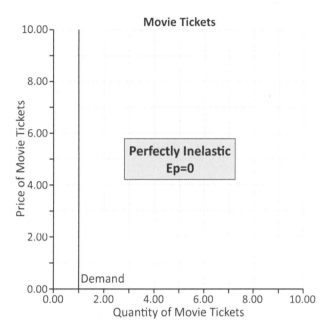

B. If we go to the $5.00 matinee, I will take my girlfriend and her 3 sisters. If we go in the evening for $7, it will be just the two of us.

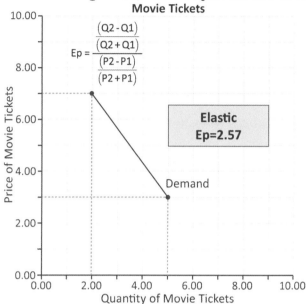

C. I bought a Costco gift card and will spend $25 on going to the movies.

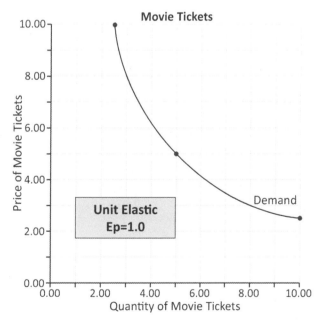

D. I will always take my girlfriend to the movies, as long as the price isn't over $9.75

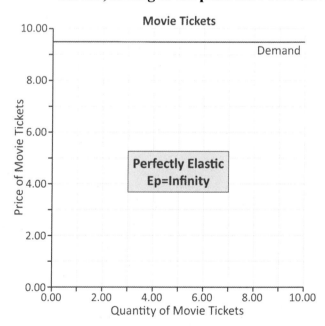

Question 6: U2 just came out with a new album. They have been selling 10,000 CDs a month at $15.00. Since Coldplay is also releasing a new album, U2 is considering selling their CD at $13.00. U2 hired an economist and found the price elasticity of demand to be (–) 1.5 over the relevant range.

A. Graph the question.

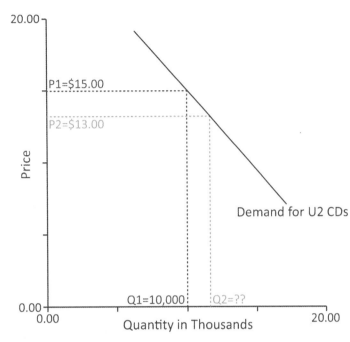

B. How many CDs should U2 expect to sell if they change the price?

$$1.5 = \frac{\%\Delta QD}{\%\Delta P}$$

P1 : $15.00   Q1 : 10,000   TR1 : $150,000
P2 : $13.00   **Q2 : ??**   **TR2 : ??**

$$\%\Delta P \;\rightarrow\; \frac{\$15.00 - \$13.00}{\$15.00} \;\rightarrow\; \frac{\$2.00}{\$15.00} \;\rightarrow\; \frac{1}{7.5} \;\rightarrow\; 0.1333$$

$$1.5 = \frac{\%\Delta QD}{0.1333} \;\rightarrow\; 1.5 \times (0.1333) = \%\Delta QD \;\rightarrow\; 0.2 = \%\Delta QD$$

Check : $1.5 = \dfrac{0.2}{0.1333}$

We **know** the change in QD = .2 (or 20%), therefore the new quantity demanded after the decrease in price will be: 10,000 + 20% or **12,000 units**.

C. Use total revenue to explain if this is a good economic decision.

Total Revenue 1: $15.00 * 10,000 = $150,000
Total Revenue 2: $13.00 * 12,000 = $156,000

Since **Total Revenue increases**, we know this is a good economic decision and U2 should decrease the price of the CDs to $13.00

Question 7: The Oakland A's and the San Francisco Giants are two Major League Baseball teams that have ballparks located with in 16 miles of each other. The San Francisco Giants are currently selling 20,000 club level seats at $35.00 each for their home games. The Oakland A's were selling their club level seats for $25.00, but are going to reduce the price to $20.00. An economist found the cross-price elasticity to be 3.0 between the two team's club level seats.

A. Graph the given information.

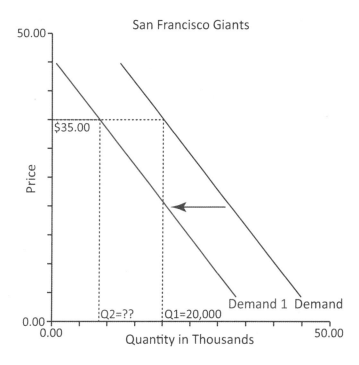

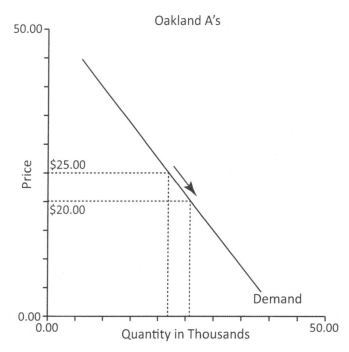

B. Calculate how many seats the SF Giants should expect to sell with the A's new price.

$$Exy = 3.0 \rightarrow \frac{\%\Delta QD(SF)}{\%\Delta P(A's)} \qquad \begin{array}{ll} (SF)Q1 : 20,000 & (A's)P1 : \$25.00 \\ \textbf{(SF)Q2 : ??} & (A's)P2 : \$20.00 \end{array}$$

$$3.0 = \frac{\dfrac{Q2 - Q1}{Q1}}{\dfrac{P2 - P1}{P1}} \rightarrow 3.0 = \frac{\dfrac{Q2 - 20,000}{20,000}}{\dfrac{\$20.00 - \$25.00}{\$25.00}} \rightarrow 3.0 = \frac{\dfrac{Q2 - 20,000}{20,000}}{\dfrac{-\$5.00}{\$25.00}} \rightarrow$$

$$3.0 = \frac{\dfrac{Q2 - 20,000}{20,000}}{-\dfrac{1}{5}} \rightarrow \frac{\dfrac{Q2 - 20,000}{20,000}}{-0.2} \rightarrow 3.0(-0.2) = \frac{Q2 - 20,000}{20,000} \rightarrow$$

$$-0.6(20,000) = Q2 - 20,000 \rightarrow -12,000 = Q2 - 20,000 \rightarrow 8,000 = Q2$$

C. Use the coefficient to explain how these two goods are related.

If the Cross-Price elasticity is a positive number, we know that the two goods are substitutes. With a number as large as 3.0, we know the goods are viewed as very close substitutes.

Question 8: Wally's World of Widgets hires you as their full time economist. After studying their business, you realize that when the price of Widgets are $50.00 they sell 20,000 units a month and when they put Widgets on sale for $35.00 they sell 10,000 units more a month.

A. Graph the given information.

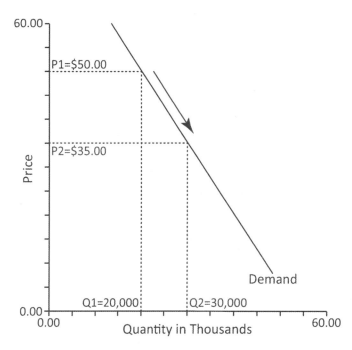

B. What is the arc elasticity over the relevant range? What does this number mean?

P1 : $50.00   Q1 : 20,000
P2 : $35.00   Q2 : 30,000

$$\text{Arc Elasticity} = \frac{\dfrac{\Delta QD}{\text{Average QD}}}{\dfrac{\Delta P}{\text{Average P}}} \rightarrow \frac{\dfrac{10}{\left[\dfrac{(20,000+30,000)}{2}\right]}}{\dfrac{15}{\left[\dfrac{(\$50+\$35)}{2}\right]}} \rightarrow \frac{0.4}{0.3529} \rightarrow \mathbf{1.1334}$$

A price elasticity of 1.1334 means that for every 1% decrease in price, we know that quantity demanded will go up 1.134%.

C. Use total revenue to explain if this is a good economic decision.

TR1: $1,000,000
TR2: $1,050,000

Since total revenue has increased by $50,000, this is a good economic decision.

Question 1: Use the graph to answer the following questions. All labels have been removed, but you can assume that the supply and demand curves are the same ones that we have been working with for most of the semester, you can also assume that the axis are the ones that we typically have used (price is in dollars and quantity is in thousands).

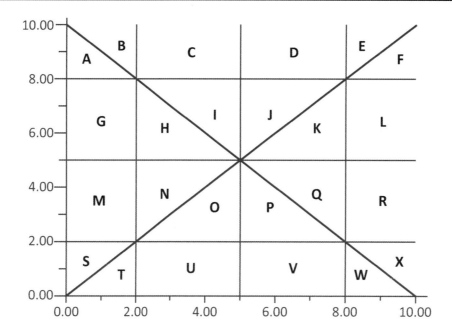

In equilibrium, what are the letters and the total dollar amounts that correspond to the area for the...

   i. Original Consumer Surplus?

  ii. Original Producer Surplus?

 iii. Total Market Surplus?

Assume an effective quota has been placed on the market, changing the quantity by 3,000 units. What are the letters and the total dollar amounts that now correspond to the...

  iv. New Consumer Surplus?

   v. New Producer Surplus?

  vi. Area that was transferred?

 vii. Dead Weight Loss?

viii. Remaining Surplus?

In equilibrium, what are the letters and the total dollar amounts that correspond to the area for the…

i. Original Consume Surplus? AGH ½ ($5)(5,000) = **$12,500**

ii. Original Producer Surplus? MNS ½ ($5)(5,000) = **$12,500**

iii. Total Market Surplus? AGH + MNS = $12,500 + $12,500 = **$25,000**

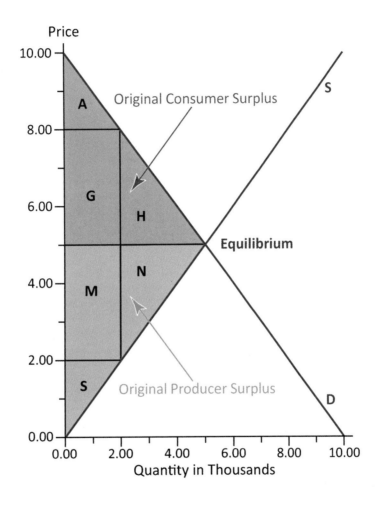

Assume an effective quota has been placed on the market, changing the quantity by 3,000 units. What are the letters and the total dollar amounts that now correspond to the...

iv. New Consumer Surplus?   A →   ½ ($2)(2,000) = **$2,000**

v. New Producer Surplus?   GMS →   ($3*2,000) + ($3*2,000) + [½ ($2*2,000)] = **$14,000**

vi. Area that was transferred? G →   ($3*2,000) = **$6,000**

vii. Dead Weight Loss?   HN →   [½ ($3*3,000)]+ [½ ($3*3,000)] = **$9,000**

viii. Remaining Surplus?   AGMS→ $16,000 or $25,000 – $9,000 = **$16,000**

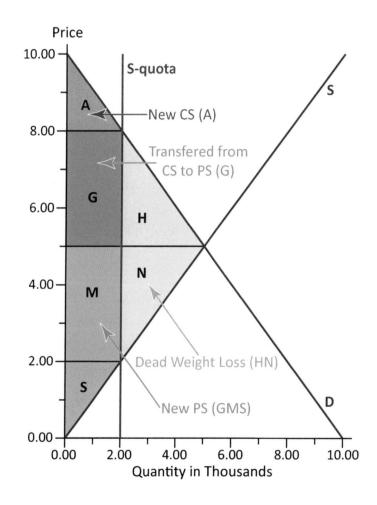